God's Harvest

A Book of Poetry

by Michelle Lynn Swope

edited by Cheryl Swope, M.Ed.

*Dedicated to all special-needs
children, teens, adults, and older folks ...*

This is our story, of poems and a light—
the light of childhood with moments that never
grow old, never dim, never fade and never die.

Yours truly,

Michelle Lynn Swope

GOD'S HARVEST:
A Book of Poetry

by Michelle Lynn Swope
edited by Cheryl Swope, M.Ed.

ISBN 978-1-61538-890-5

Contents

Acknowledgments

Thank you to Tanya Charlton, Jessica Osborne, and Jennifer Farrior of Memoria Press for the beautiful design work and final copy editing. I appreciate your hard and dedicated work in bringing this book to life.

Special thanks to my friend and fellow author, Mrs. Katie Schuermann, for her encouragement to complete this collection:

> What words, what thoughts,
> Art thy crown.
> Beauteous speech renown.

To my honored parents

Thank you for the time you spent, the materials you used, and for driving us to libraries and museums when you could have been doing other things. For all the time, toil, tears, and hours of Shakespeare and Latin, I humbly and sincerely give you this milestone of my second poetry book with a hearty shout out, and a very well done.

Michelle

A Word to My Readers

To my audience, whom I tenderly address:

I hope and express my thoughts to you with these offerings and outpourings. Take them as thou wilt. They are spoken, given from the heart, and each stand and beat as one.

This collection of love, of sorrow, of joy, of light, of tears to shake away heartache, is to bring hope to the world ashambles.

Music, religion, songs of joy in the sinner's ear,
What mercy did God write and bring!
Amen! Amen! Let the praises ring
To Christ be glory, and to Him angels sing.

Michelle

Heartfelt Prayers & Religion

God's Harvest

Long be the harvest great
And every wood and grain,
Be gentle when the sowers reap
That plenty in the harvest keep.

Raise Harvest

Golden sunbeams across the fields,
Blessings fall within the yield.
Come what might,
Fullness or blight.

Hay in the meadow,
Cows in the field,
God's design
In harvest wield.

Cotton, fiber, soybean, husks,
God's own Son died for us.
Sinners gather to the Word.
Sunshine rays; blessings heard.

Plea

Lord God of heaven above,
Pray we now in heartfelt love.
Beg we now in highest praise,
Plead we now Your tender aid.

Give comfort, help in time of trial,
Spare this now Your humble child.
In Jesus' name we ask this now …
Amen! Amen! Amen!

Serenity

A clock tower chimes
An unearthly spell.
Day be done
As night falls.

Night shades the hill,
Shadows everywhere.
Gloom yet not doom
Shall take us.

Sabbath is nigh.
God's praise is Thine,
Everlasting to everlasting
Peace recline.

Allies

Written after church one day, age 19

Although my tears were seconded,
The motion was in vain.
Happiness in clearest frame
Only did He deign.
Truest form is known;
The Sinless overcame.

Arise

For each earthly instance
Sin must surely pay.
A breath, a drop
Upon the river all must stop.

But open the gateway
to Heaven slides.
The farther shore
Appointed, arrives.

Challenge

Race on; battle's won.
Fight ye the good fight of Faith.
Stricken, smitten, know ye well,
Like Him, fight! Fight!

Ye conquerors old,
Worn, tired, lost,
Brave and bold,
Jesus comes into the fray.

Lost, until Him this very day …
Strike! Blow by biting blow,
Nothing's lost;
For us, Jesus they assault.

Heavenly homeward is our course,
In Jesus we rejoice!

Misery

Misery what chains
To heavy extent you bring.
Heaven help us break your power
Within the earthen store.

In joy and peace,
Mercy do You bring.
Sorrow late, come what might
        Earth no reason great.

Still

Every man for the world is sold
Lines a confessional pew.

Every man in the world
Taunted Christ the Jew.

Every man sick an' sore
Calling out to God.

Jesus, Father, Savior, Man of War,
Come to save us all.

Storm

Oh, God, now thunder roars
The tender rain outpours.
Gently streaming, never ceasing,
Oh the sky downpours.

Gentle sobbing as the sun
Sets slowly in the west,
People doubting, sky arising;
Only dawn will fortify.

For You

Written in gratitude to Mrs. Jill Roth, my gentle overseer at work

See this tree, was it for me,
God of grace and Lord of might.
Deep in thought reserved for me,
Only good I see in Thee.

Lord of lords and King of kings
We bow in meet humility.
Soft in spread and tall in bough,
God has made a special call.

For you, for me, He did indeed,
Die upon the cursed tree.
For us He laid His glory down,
Victor's rest and Victor's crown.

Notions

Dedicated to Dr. Gene Edward Veith

Hell—by no means can man
Deliver himself from sin.
From most early age
Death's whitish peel hath us in its grasp.

Time only tells eternity,
And with its toll comes age.
Man was once a great work,
Soon to be again
In the blood of the Lamb.

Mortification

Why am I buried in all this lace?
Questionable is this questionable race,
Must all below answer
God's good grace.

When the last have spoken
And shut their mouths,
What is it to have ears,
Yet mourn the dead?

Time and fashion here at hand,
When all below in the land
Must think hard and must think fast,
Or Jubilee simply won't last.

Trespasses

Oh, forgive me, Lord,
For I have sinned
And gone astray;
Bless me now I pray …

Long have I been absent, Lord,
From this place You call home.
Father, Abba, give me grace.
To You, Trinity, I now trace.

Jesus, Lord, for us He pleads,
Granting grace, supplying needs.

Wisdom

Wisdom's words
Full of cheer
Breaketh noon,
A noonday spear.

Mapping all but wisdom's ways,
Judging paths in error's maze.

Manna

Our Father who from heaven
Sent down appealing love,
Bread first gave, home applaud,
Light and Love appeals to all,
Joys unceasing, doubts console.

Jesu, "Peace," says unto all.
Sin for us came to destroy,
Love empowers us to say,
"Jesus loves us, death he slays.
Keep us in the narrow way."

Please for us, we humbly beg,
Send us now some heavenly Bread.
By Your power on us descend,
By Your love our death unsend.

Thine the Glory

For Thine the glory,
Thine the power,
Forever and ever,
Amen.

Oh, Christ the Lamb,
From within Thine hand
Peace and joy
Extend.

Apology

I am sorry …

Though I know no words to say.
I was wrong.
May it be in better light arrayed.

Captive were my deeds and ways.
Deep in doubt was I,
Deep in sin.

Debts

Assume we the poorest of the lot,
Beggers, filth, and stench.
To us and to our inheritance
Death comes, our lot.

To be honest, look at me,
Tired, pale, and wan.
The offenses borne for me, for you,
Christ, the eternal boon.

Forgive us our debts, as
We forgive our trespassers.
Mercy, we beg thee,
Oh, Lord.

Preserve and approve,
Forgive and forget.
Debts we all must pay:
Forgiven, forgotten … Say!

The Magnificat

Herald calls
The day is done.
Light unceasing falls.
Praises now unfailing gives
Elizabeth, Mary, John.

Sin came to a gracious King,
Life and love to sinners heave.
Though we may wander far,
Jesu is the calling star.

Thy Kingdom Come

In words and thoughts and plights
We humbly beg and pray.
Thy kingdom come,
    Thy will be done,
We come to you this day.

Here on earth and in heaven,
Share and share alike
Prayers unspoken, debts unpaid,
    Curses laid
Upon the back of Christ.

For sinful people God's own Son
Came and gave His life.
Strikes and spit
    God's derelict;
Only gift: His Love.

Memories

Mommy Cake

Written one night for my mom when she was sick

A spoonful of sugar,
A pound of spice,
Two full eggs,
That's twice as nice.

A pinch of nutmeg,
One whole clove,
A cup full of nectar,
And a pound of love.

Winter Weather

Winter dawns so clear, so swift
Softly in the light.
Winter shadows dawn at eve,
Crisp the winter's night.

Fallen snow chills the air,
Breathes the winter sprite.
Soft and sweet, drifts petite
On a winter's night.

As I Dreamed to Be

As I dreamed to be:
Long, long ago,
In fancies sweet,
In dreams of yore,
Passing, fleeting,
Leaving, … Oh!
Flying by, like a shooting star.

As I wish in dreams tonight …
A kiss good night.
In my heart I wish tonight,
Running theme,
Dwelling hither, as an art
From day to night,
And back it bends:

Daddy's little girl,
A wife to become.

Air

Air, give me room to breathe,
A breath of air roams free.
Sweet summer sunshine,
Cool fall rain,
Winter's chilling breeze,
Droplets' cooling freeze.

To slush, to slush away,
The winter flies.
Give me a breath of air
Before winter's demise.

"Give me air,"
A simple mind cries,
And on happier days,
Spring on the wind will rise.

The Wishing Well

In remembrance of my favorite rock wishing well at the St. Louis Zoo,
known to me from age 3 until it was removed, 1998-2014

How oft I know this wishing well,
And sigh for it in vain.
The tears run courses o'er, and are
Often very much plain.

To be or not 'tis that,
I very much ask at all,
As my dear little wishing well,
Sighs and grows so small.

I shudder to think who ordered this,
Left my dear little well
Changed and abandoned,
Forgotten, misshapen,
The little wishing well of yore!

Thanksgiving

Written after Thanksgiving dinner at Grandpa and Noni's

The night is fleeting
'Ere we leave the banquet hall.
A little turkey, some stuffing near,
Rolls and casseroles galore.

We're all God's children here,
Family too,
And these are things we should be thankful for:
Family, food, and all things good.

Party

Welcome to my web,
Where fiery orbs yet glow.
Listen to the rain falling,
As they flow.

Smoke blows, curling high
Up into the trees.
Birds sing their finest
Good night melodies.

Higher still
In the forest tall,
The leaves sway
In the forest primeval.

Like young men with fiery thoughts
For young damsels under pain,
Welcome to my web,
Where thoughts are all the same.

Grandsire

Written at the passing of my 90-year-old grandfather, and read at his graveside

Fades of sunshine,
Tears of laughter,
Spoken wisdom on the tongue,
Beckons too, the world of God.

Heaven's eve has called him,
Blessed saint before the throne.
Round with all the holy angels,
Beckons, welcome home.

Welcome home the little lamb …
Welcome home this blessed child.

Independence Day

When woe befell our fathers, Lord,
With all but errant grace afford,
With time and prayers and tears on earth,
All would understand the dearth.

"To arms, to arms," we hear the cry:
Men fall in blood and earth to die.
To us and them they understand,
The meaning: sacrifice.

Wonderland

Snow of garlands,
Ice of tears,
Come to me
In winter's tiers.

Years have fallen;
Snow has come.
Why, oh why,
Am I undone?

Teardrops glisten
On the page,
Frost that sparkles
On with age.

Time and time
I speak with pain,
Why, oh why,
Am I ashamed?

Snow has fallen,
Whispers over head,
"Come unto me;
It's time for bed."

The Source of Sweet Music

Deep within my mind's eye
I see the Sainte Genevieve railroad flashing by.
I hear within my mind's ear
The song of fiddles twanging clear,
The song of maidens loud and dear,
The song, the song of yesteryear.

March On
Written for my quaint hometown

March on, march on
·Till day is done,
Till strife is won.

March on, march on.
God is by thy side.

Till day is done
And battle won,
March on, Sainte Genevieve, march on.

Magic

Magic has taught us to believe
In oneself to achieve,
To comment on one's blessings,
Yea or nay indeed.

Alpha and Omega, here to stay.
Stones and pits, will have no sway,
Grinding cheek and splitting hay,
Where oft has magic come to stay?

Heavenly chords do no wrong,
Truer chimes sound to the throng.

Uncle Stuart
Written for the funeral of my dad's little brother

Dear friends, dear one and all,
We're gathered here this day,
We're joined in sight of sadness,
Death appalls; dismay.

Mourn we now this gentle man,
Brother, uncle, friend.
Baptized in Christ, a man can live
Smiling without end.

Danielle

Written upon the death of my singing friend, Danielle. The untimely death
of my friend recalls to mind that of another young lady, pictured in the
painting below.

In soft we meet in paradise,
A bird of fledgling thou;
Flies high away, our tears we shed,
No more in pain allow.

The good-byes said,
Sadly you are gone,
But we shall miss and remember still
Our kin, the bird of paradise until …

Rose Blossoms

Rose blossoms slip and slide
Through the rain.
Through many a drip, many a drop,
Many a shower, rain poureth over.

Rose blossoms awaken in the night
And cometh out in full array
In the morning.

Retirees
Written for two nurses retiring after 16 years of service from the
Ste. Genevieve Care Center

Up like a bird,
Your old job flown,
Your new one found
Fair above ground.

Must we with tears
Bid you adieu,
So long, good luck
Be with you.

My Home

In memory of the family lake house, where memories grew on trees!

Oh dear and oh, away you fly!
Away, away, beyond the sky.
Still past my hopes and dreams –
Never more!

The times we spent,
The hours went,
Within your hallowed halls
We lived.

The teardrops shed
At your departure wed,
Oh the aches and tears
To see you a former friend of many years.

But now the gentle hour is past.
Our friend has a new owner at last.

Still it is to be grieved
When at last we must leave
The dear old lakehouse,
My home of memories!

Rose

A rose blooms or falls
Like many an autumn day.
Death takes its toll,
Sharpens many to desire.

Fate dons a mask
That no one ever sees.
Fate brings the many falling,
Falling to their knees.

Love &
Ballads

The Wandering Prince

Timid, shy, the night arrives,
Wide with wondering surprise.
A day, a night, you meet the prince;
He asks you now to dance.

You make a bow, a timid bow,
And answer gladly, "Yes."
You stand before the company,
And you begin to dance.

It looks today from the way they say,
That you are a couple, yes.
You reply to the prince simply,
Dancing in your best.

So if reality, my friend,
A night at the ball has you,
Dancing in each other's arms,
May you both have a happy ever after?
Yes, yes, yes!

Bells

Hear the bells call
At the close of today.
Hear the birds sing
In the twilight of day.

See a young maid
And a young man
Stand watching the sun
Both hand in hand.

Wedding Feast

Stir the cup
And prime the hall,
Fancy feathers all do call.

Stir the pot
And knead the dough,
Fancy wading through the snow.

Amid the hours
Midnight falls,
Dancing couples await the ball.

Thankfulness

Dedicated to Mr. Rick and Mrs. Karen (Schulte) Fields with thanks for kind hospitality

Blessings be upon this house
Where hospitality reigns.
Where love and friends gather,
And rudeness has no gain.

Generosity, kindness, courtesy,
Meet on these special days,
Where all in all are welcomed here,
Gentleness all can claim.

Mother

Written to our wonderful mother on Valentine's Day

Swifter than the stars above,
Like the twinkling lights,
Many an air dustmote falls,
Like a spark in the night.

Air seemeth more than hue,
As many seem to say:
What twinkles now, what says again:
Happy Valentine's Day!

Shadows

Written at age 17, song composed of lost love

Way out past the sunset,
Way out past the sea,
Shining moon and shadows
Are not close to thee.

Farther than the wind blows,
Farther than the waves,
Roars upon the sandbrakes,
Closer to my face.

Though I am sailing
Farther out to sea,
Closer than a mile,
Closer now to thee.

I see thee not, as I am
Farther than the tide,
Deeper than the waters,
Swift as light.

Child

Pitter patter of little feet
Dance across the floor.
Sorrows, joys, and daydreams
Now are no more.

A gust of wind, a shadow,
The morrow brings to say:
Remorse, sadness, joy surrender
All there ever was to pay.

Night falls as she rises,
The Savior lends a hand.
"Talitha cumi, young lady,
Rise and live again."

Old Woman

See this old woman, all trimmed in lace,
God's creation sent from a heavenly race.
Old woman now, 'ere shown from above
God's time, God's pleasure, God's gracious love.

This old woman, fair not to see,
This old woman born of the free.
This old woman made free to stand,
Born of Christ and of the land.

Maiden I: A Ballad

Written at age 18 as a gift for Mother's Day

The young piper had oft been told, for a lofty seat
and ring of gold, that he must pipe and tell the
story of the maiden well:

High in the skies ahead,
Lo in the earth unwed,
Lived a maiden on the glistening green
With her hero true.

But high in the skies above,
Lived there cunning and blue,
An archer god who loved
This same maiden too.

The god became so bold,
He wished the hero dead.
"Fairest maid shall never live
    by hero's side,"
The wicked god then said.

In pride and in lust,
He fought war and main,
But not fairly sought
Was the endwise of his game.

Outspake the maiden
Wisely and true,
"If the god shouldst have a challenge,
Let them answer you."

"If death, then let the price be me.
For what is death? An omen,
And the price is but a gift."

"You hear my challenge,
Oh god of archer and of sky,
What say you to my resume?"

The god spoke thus from the heaven,
"I like it much, fair maid.
While yonder weep beyond the deep,
I'll have you by my side today."

The hero tried to dissuade her
In words more full and grand,
"Please my sweet, please do retreat
Come, and take my hand."

But lo, the maiden waved him off.
"Duty must be done.
I'll keep my word,
As honor is establishment."

She chastened then,
"Go away, you coward be,
I am not afraid of death!"

The fair maiden sits in the stars,
The archer god is by her side,
No longer blue but full of joy
To have triumphed o'er the man
And left the royal court a'weeping.

The young piper finishes trilling as he does,
Of maiden's death and ascension to the stars
To sit with the archer god.

So he piped most beautifully,
And as he did most well,
An official seat in government,
Rich robes and a ring of gold,
Were given to the young piper,
For this story that he told.

The Talisman of the King: A Ballad
Bedtime tale without rhyme

An old man lay dying now upon his wearied bed,
Says he, "Many's the day I've striven to keep land
and title free.
My daughter's wed, my son abed, and so soon am
I to die?
Then 'fore my God I come content," and thus the
old man died.

An aged man rides around with a pinched look on
his face.
His daughter's of an age to wed and eager, but
none can take the place.
To he, the young girl's father, death will soon
carry him off.
"Curses," spake the king, "for were I but young
once more,
I'd marry off my daughter, save her well, and save
her from this hell."

"Nay," returneth his gentle squire at last, "You are
what you are,
Oh reverent sire, and naught can dissuade fate's
spell.
Indeed, if I had rank and title, I'd myself try for the
lovely lady's hand.
But seeing I have neither, I'll serve her other ways
as best I can."

The king returned so jovially, "You love her,
    my lad!"
The squire said, "I cannot lie; I will speak but
    truth, and say I do."
The king spake, "Then I hereby make you a knight
Worthy of my daughter, the princess true."

So the pair were wed and blessed by the king,
They spent many a year together.
Buried at each other's side,
They remained together when they died.

Childhood brings back so many memories of a
    little girl and boy,
Playing in meadows, playing in the market,
    down by the river, over by the stables,
Sometime together, often alone, they grew year
    by year
In training of what they would become:
    Daughter, princess, queen, wife, mother
    Squire, prince, king, husband, father

They shared the bond of unity now and
    forever more,
Their children became very special
Of important reign known all over the world.
So, children, that is their tale.
Now I am off for bed,

And you, too, must now rest.
Good men close their eyes
In the dead of night, 'tis best.
Now so must you.

Exit Grannie, who told the bedtime tale.

The Soldier: A Ballad

On foreign land
The soldier stands,
Wishing once for home.
Duty is as duty done,
So forth he makes no sound.

Across the world and far from home
In lands in inky blue,
He's fought and fought
And fought some more
In the untimely hue.

So sad was he, so sad was he
The day he fought with might,
He took the gamble,
Then at last,
He paid the final price.

Alone and unafraid he died
To save a comrade-in-arms.
On enemy shore,
Death was inevitable,
He must come to harm.

So far from his fiancee Grace,
In turn they themselves
Became the lost,
For the lost to save.

All mourn a loss, 'tis so,
One price paid; full woe.
Bravest hero, bold to die,
Alone now told,
His sacrifice.

Mary and Martha

God calls us to understand
How brief this life has been.
His Word, His Law He's written,
Our hearts, our souls within.

Mary, God's good friend,
Sat and heard His teaching begin.
Martha, house to style, just then
Rudely called her sister in.
"Is it mine to serve alone
Before our Master
Is thin like bone?"

Gently Jesus calls to her:
Martha, Martha, you begin
To see what style the world is in.
Mary stays; God's love resides.

Mary, Martha, two apart,
God calls us His
Love to impart.

Just for Fun

ABCs and 123s

This is the first poem I ever created. My mom says I sang this song often at age 2, and it came out the same every time.

ABCs and 123s,
'Bout to bee a frenzy dooker,
Andy handy boober's,
One too find a threeber's,
Andy handy boober's!

My Valentine

A poem written as if from my dad to my mom

Once do I recall
That same sad sound,
Wishing you were near.

Along came a miss,
Then I happened to trip
And looked up from on the floor.

Lo, you were with me here,
My love, my angel, my sweet.

Prostrating myself
In this inelegant attitude,
Was not very stylish nor flattering …

As I stood up, regaining my mind,
I drank my cup of tea,
Gazed into your eyes and saw only you:

You, my darling wife!

Fish on the Sea

Fish on the sea,
And fish on the land,
Where do they end up,
But in the frying pan.

For crying aloud,
Oh give me a break,
Help send the fish
Back into the lake!

Air Space

Time is of the essence
Where no man sees,
Air, beach, earth
Just for me …

Time ages on
In manner be,
Fish of the ocean
Swim to the sea …

Afterword

Let these things here lie forthwith
For all the world's due, One remits.
Not as mere rock nor as mere flame,
Nothing in due course, the earth retains.

Let all these things sleep under the sky,
For all until all no longer lie,
Till Jesus Lord and Lord of all
Sounds His mighty trumpet call.

Let all who believe, rejoice today.
Cast all your cares away.
Take hold firm grasp to keep
Eternal Joy's good sleep.

Michelle

Made in the USA
Coppell, TX
16 March 2022